MY FIRST

GREEN
B·O·O·K

Angela Wilkes

DK

DORLING KINDERSLEY
London • New York • Stuttgart

A Dorling Kindersley Book

Design Mathewson Bull
Photography Dave King and Mike Dunning
Editor Andrea Pinnington
Production Norina Bremner

Art Director Roger Priddy

First published in Great Britain in 1991
by Dorling Kindersley Limited,
9 Henrietta Street, London WC2E 8PS

**A CIP catalogue record for this book
is available from the British Library**

ISBN 0-86318-623-8

Phototypeset by Setting Studio, Newcastle
Colour reproduction by Colourscan, Singapore
Printed and bound in Italy by L.E.G.O.

Dorling Kindersley would like to thank Jonathan Buckley,
Helen Drew, Mandy Earey, Marie Greenwood, Ann Kramer,
Steve Parker and Stephen Webster for their help
in producing this book.

Illustrations by Brian Delf

CONTENTS

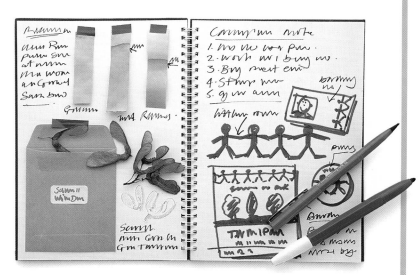

BEING GREEN

Being green does not mean changing colour. It means caring about our environment and trying to change some of the things we do so that we stop harming and polluting the world around us. The Earth is facing massive problems at the moment, but everyone can do something to help. First though, we have to understand what the problems are. This is what **My First Green Book** sets out to do.

World problems

There are many problems facing our planet. The air is no longer clean to breathe. Rivers, seas and the countryside are polluted. Tropical rainforests are being chopped down. Plants and animals are dying out. And we are using up the Earth's supply of fossil fuels, such as oil and coal. **My First Green Book** explains what many of these problems actually mean. It also suggests things that you can do to help put the problems right. Everything that you do, no matter how small, has an effect on the world around you.

Look around you

Being green starts at home. Look at how much the car is used for unnecessary journeys. Look at exactly what your family buys at the shops every week. Once you are aware of what is going on around you, you can try to cut down on waste. That is being green.

Where you live

Once you have started being green at home, you can turn your attention to the place where you live. How safe is it to cycle there? Are there any local litter or recycling schemes? Start a green diary, so that you can make notes of the things you find out.

Action

One of the best ways to help do something about green issues is to join an environmental organization. You can get their addresses at your public library. Or you can set up a campaign group with your friends. Children can help to make the world a better place. The future of the Earth is in your hands!

GREEN EXPERIMENTS

My First Green Book is full of fascinating projects and experiments to do at home that will help you to understand some of the environmental problems facing our planet. Step-by-step photographs and simple instructions show you exactly what to do, and there are life-size photographs of everything you need to collect and of the finished projects. On the opposite page is a list of things to read before you start. Below are the points to look for in each experiment.

How to use this book

The things you need
The things to collect for each experiment are shown life-size, to help you check that you have everything you need.

Equipment
These illustrated checklists show you which equipment to have ready before you start an experiment.

Step-by-step
Step-by-step photographs and clear instructions show you what to do at each stage of the experiment.

JAM JAR LID TEST
You can set up this very simple experiment at home to find out just how clean or dirty the air is where you live. The experiment takes a week to do, so be patient. You have to set up the equipment outside, but remember to bring it inside at the first sign of rain, as water will spoil the result of your experiment.

EQUIPMENT

Small labels

Pen (or pencil)

You will need

A sheet of white card

7 jam jar lids or bottle tops

Setting up the experiment

1 Write the numbers one to seven on the card, as shown. Stick labels to the jam jar lids and number them from one to seven.

2 Lay the jam jar lids on the card, matching the numbers. Then put the card and the lids outside in a sheltered place.

3 Leave the card outside for a week. At the end of the first day, take away lid number one. Each day take away one more lid.

The seventh day
At the end of the week, take away the last lid. If the air is dirty, the patches where the first lids were will be darker than the others.

SPECKS OF DIRT
The experiment works best if you live in a large town or city. The air is dirtier there because of all the vehicles, chimneys and factories. How often do your windows need cleaning, or your car?

HOW YOU CAN HELP
• Use the car less. Ride a bicycle or use public transport.
• Turn off lights and don't waste hot water. The less gas and electricity we use, the less fuel power stations burn and the less pollution they cause.

10

11

Things to remember

1 Read the instructions before you start and gather together everything you need for the experiment.

2 Put on an apron or old shirt and roll up your sleeves. Cover your work table with newspaper.

3 Follow the instructions carefully at each stage of the experiment and only do one thing at a time.

4 Be very careful with sharp scissors. **Do not use them unless there is an adult there to help you.**

5 Keep a record of each experiment or project and its results in your green diary (see page 44).

6 When you have finished, put everything away, clean up any mess and wash your hands.

The final results
Life-size photographs show you what happens at the end of the experiment, so that you know what to expect.

Explanation
At the end of each experiment you will find a simple explanation of what has happened and why.

How you can help
Many of the experiments are followed by a list of things you can do to help improve environmental problems.

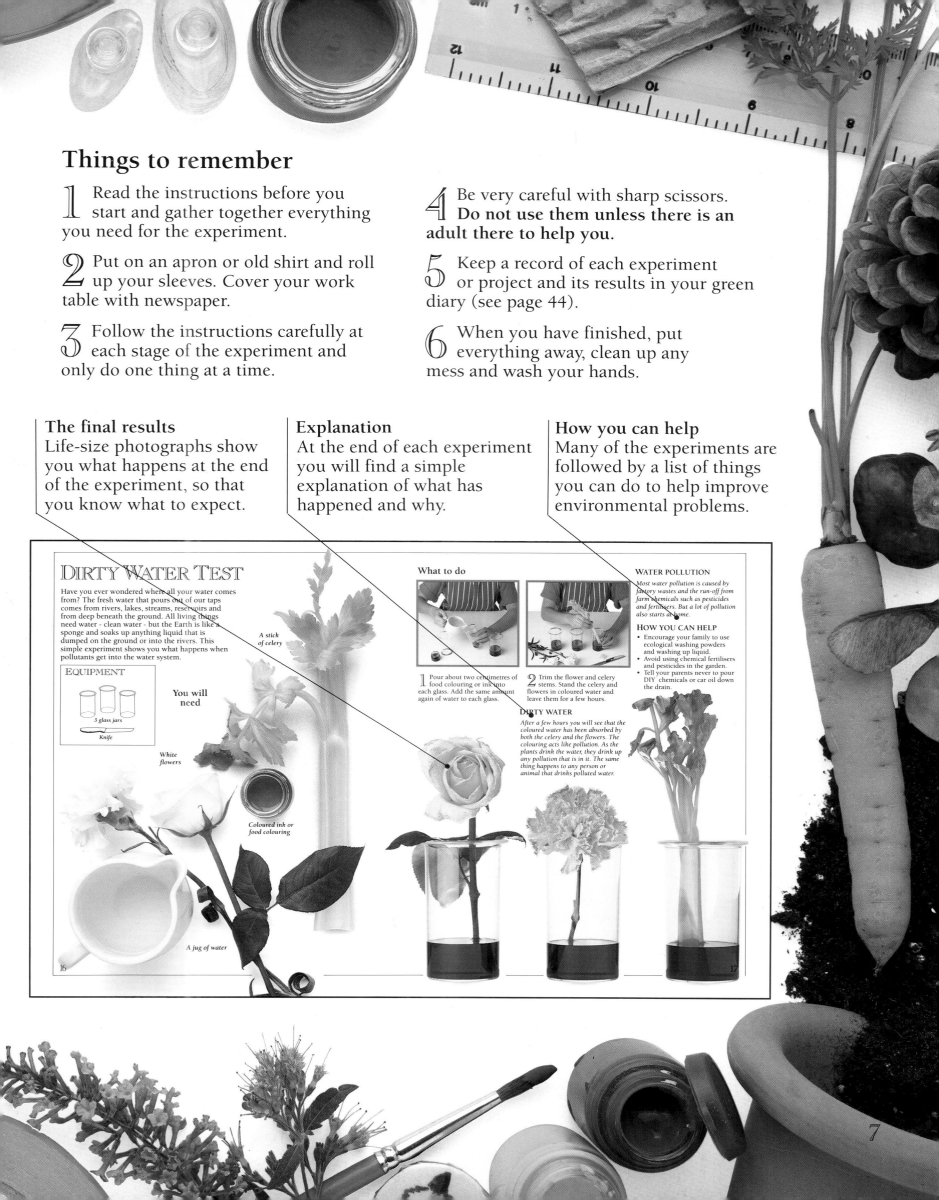

DIRTY WATER TEST

Have you ever wondered where all your water comes from? The fresh water that pours out of our taps comes from rivers, lakes, streams, reservoirs and from deep beneath the ground. All living things need water - clean water - but the Earth is like a sponge and soaks up anything liquid that is dumped on the ground or into the rivers. This simple experiment shows you what happens when pollutants get into the water system.

EQUIPMENT

3 glass jars

Knife

You will need

A stick of celery

White flowers

Coloured ink or food colouring

A jug of water

What to do

1 Pour about two centimetres of food colouring or ink into each glass. Add the same amount again of water to each glass.

2 Trim the flower and celery stems. Stand the celery and flowers in coloured water and leave them for a few hours.

DIRTY WATER

After a few hours you will see that the coloured water has been absorbed by both the celery and the flowers. The colouring acts like pollution. As the plants drink the water, they drink up any pollution that is in it. The same thing happens to any person or animal that drinks polluted water.

WATER POLLUTION

Most water pollution is caused by factory wastes and the run-off from farm chemicals such as pesticides and fertilisers. But a lot of pollution also starts at home.

HOW YOU CAN HELP
- Encourage your family to use ecological washing powders and washing up liquid.
- Avoid using chemical fertilisers and pesticides in the garden.
- Tell your parents never to pour DIY chemicals or car oil down the drain.

16

17

AIR POLLUTION

Most people assume that the air we breathe is clean, but this is not always so. Factories and power stations pour smoke and poisonous gases out into the sky as they produce electricity and goods, and vehicles belch out exhaust fumes. All these things *pollute* (make dirty) the air around us. Polluted air is bad for all living things: plants, animals and people.

You can find out how clean or dirty the air is by looking at trees, walls and stonework. Below you can see some of the signs to look for.

LICHENS

Lichens grow mainly on trees, walls and old stonework. As they have no roots or stems, lichens absorb moisture directly from the air or rain, together with any dirt that is in the air. This makes them very sensitive to air pollution. Some lichens only grow in clean air, while other hardier varieties can survive in more polluted air.

LEAFY AND HAIRY LICHENS

Leafy, green lichen like this grows on walls and trees. It is a sign that the air is quite clean. Hairy green "beard lichen" is a sign that the air is very clean.

CRUSTY ORANGE LICHEN

This sort of lichen is found on rocks or stones, such as gravestones.

Crusty orange lichen can grow in slightly polluted air.

CRUSTY GREEN LICHENS

Lichens like this grow on trees and stones. They show that the air is quite polluted.

GREEN ALGAE

Powdery green algae like this can tolerate bad pollution. If there are no lichens, but just green algae, the air is probably very dirty.

POLLUTION IN TOWNS AND CITIES

In a large city no lichens will grow at all, but you can find other signs of air pollution. Many of the buildings look grey or black, but they are not meant to. Find out what they were built from: pale stone, red or yellow brick, for example.

This broken piece of yellow London brick shows the contrast between the brick's original colour and its dirty grey surface.

CLEANING UP THE CITIES

Every year city councils spend a lot of money cleaning their buildings and monuments. Here you can see part of a large, old cathedral. The stonework on the left has been cleaned; the stonework on the right has not.

If you take a closer look at the dirty stonework, you can see the damage caused by years of air pollution and acid rain (see pages 12-15). Not only have layers of dirt built up; the harmful chemicals in the air and rain are also eating away at the stonework itself.

JAM JAR LID TEST

You can set up this very simple experiment at home to find out just how clean or dirty the air is where you live. The experiment takes a week to do, so be patient. You have to set up the equipment outside, but remember to bring it inside at the first sign of rain, as water will spoil the result of your experiment.

You will need

A sheet of white card

7 jam jar lids or bottle tops

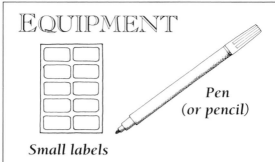

EQUIPMENT

Small labels

Pen (or pencil)

Setting up the experiment

1 Write the numbers one to seven on the card, as shown. Stick labels to the jam jar lids and number them from one to seven.

2 Lay the jam jar lids on the card, matching the numbers. Then put the card and the lids outside in a sheltered place.

3 Leave the card outside for a week. At the end of the first day, take away lid number one. Each day take away one more lid.

The seventh day

At the end of the week, take away the last lid. If the air is dirty, the patches where the first lids were will be darker than the others.

1

2

3

4

5

6

7

SPECKS OF DIRT

The experiment works best if you live in a large town or city. The air is dirtier there because of all the vehicles, chimneys and factories. How often do your windows need cleaning, or your car?

HOW YOU CAN HELP

- Use the car less. Ride a bicycle or use public transport.
- Turn off lights and don't waste hot water. The less gas and electricity we use, the less fuel power stations burn and the less pollution they cause.

RAIN CHECK

You have probably heard about acid rain, but do you really understand what it is? Here you can find out how to make litmus paper, which scientists use to test substances to see whether or not they are acidic. Then you can try making your own acid water to test. Over the page is a dramatic experiment that shows what acid rain does to plants.

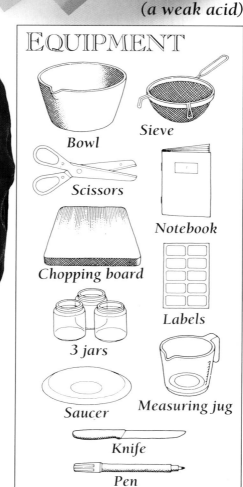

White blotting paper

Vinegar (a weak acid)

You will need

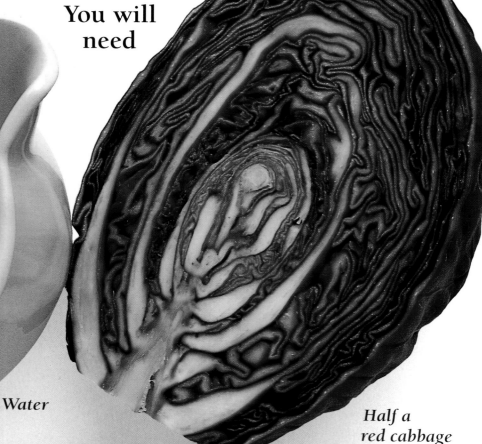

Water

Half a red cabbage

EQUIPMENT

Bowl

Sieve

Scissors

Notebook

Chopping board

Labels

3 jars

Measuring jug

Saucer

Knife

Pen

Making litmus paper

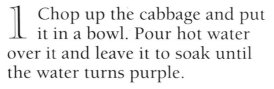

1 Chop up the cabbage and put it in a bowl. Pour hot water over it and leave it to soak until the water turns purple.

2 Hold the sieve over the jug. Pour the cabbage water into the jug through the sieve, so that the cabbage stays in the sieve.

3 Cut some small strips of blotting paper. Dip them into cabbage water, then lay them on a saucer for a few hours to dry.

The acid test

1 Pour water into one jar and label it. Pour a mixture of three quarters water and one quarter vinegar into the second jar.

2 Label the second jar *Slightly acid*. Make a mixture of half water and half vinegar in the third jar and label it *Stronger acid*.

3 Dip a strip of litmus paper into each jar. What happens to the litmus paper? Write down the results in your notebook.

WHAT HAPPENS

When you dip the litmus paper into plain water, it just darkens slightly because it is wet. But when dipped into water with vinegar in it, the litmus paper turns pink, regardless of how much vinegar is in the water.

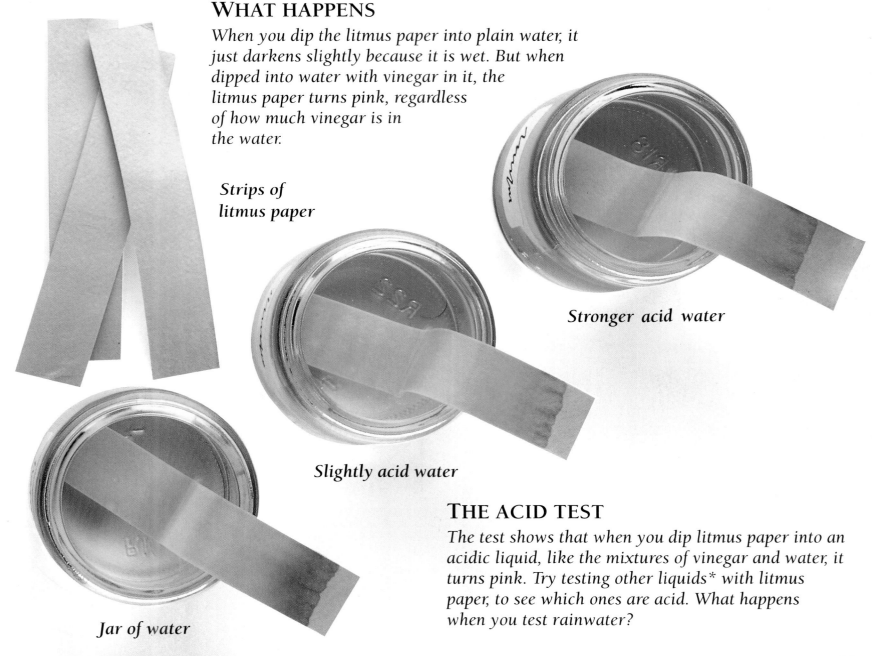

Strips of litmus paper

Stronger acid water

Slightly acid water

Jar of water

THE ACID TEST

The test shows that when you dip litmus paper into an acidic liquid, like the mixtures of vinegar and water, it turns pink. Try testing other liquids* with litmus paper, to see which ones are acid. What happens when you test rainwater?

* Check with an adult which liquids are safe to test.

ACID RAIN

All the time, poisonous gases are being released into the air from factories, power stations and vehicle exhausts. When some of these gases mix with water, they make it *acidic*. So when these gases get mixed up with rain clouds, they dissolve with the moisture in the clouds to form acid rain. Here you can find out how it affects plants.

Water

Three green plants* in pots with drip trays

You will need

Sticky labels

Vinegar

EQUIPMENT

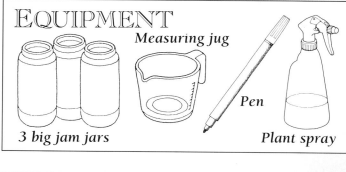

Measuring jug

Pen

3 big jam jars

Plant spray

What to do

1 Fill one of the big jars one quarter full with vinegar. Fill the remaining three quarters of the jar with water.

2 Write two labels saying *Slightly acid*. Stick one label to the jar of water and vinegar and the other to one of the plant pots.

3 Fill another big jar with water. Write two labels saying *Water*. Stick one to the jar and the other to a plant pot.

* These should be plants you can allow to die.

ACID RAIN

Acid rain has the same effect on plants as water and vinegar mixed together, but it is weaker and works more slowly. Acid rain is killing forests, poisoning lakes, harming wildlife and affecting people's health. Everyone can help to stop it.

HOW YOU CAN HELP

- Demand for electricity is the main cause of acid rain, so turn off lights.
- Use cars less.
- Recycle things.

4 Fill the remaining jar with a mixture of half water and half vinegar. Label this and the third plant pot *Stronger acid.*

5 Stand the plants in a row. Every day water and spray each one with the mixture from the jar that matches its label.

What happens

The plant that receives clean water remains strong and healthy, but the two other plants soon die. The stronger the acid, the sooner a plant dies.

Healthy green plant

This plant is dying.

This plant has already died.

Water

Slightly acid

Strong acid

DIRTY WATER TEST

Have you ever wondered where all your water comes from? The fresh water that pours out of our taps comes from rivers, lakes, streams, reservoirs and from deep beneath the ground. All living things need water - clean water - but the Earth is like a sponge and soaks up anything liquid that is dumped on the ground or into the rivers. This simple experiment shows you what happens when pollutants get into the water system.

EQUIPMENT

3 glass jars

Knife

You will need

A stick of celery

White flowers

Coloured ink or food colouring

A jug of water

What to do

HOW YOU CAN HELP

- Encourage your family to use ecological washing powders and washing up liquid.
- Avoid using chemical fertilisers and pesticides in the garden.
- Tell your parents never to pour DIY chemicals or car oil down the drain.

1 Pour about two centimetres of food colouring or ink into each glass. Add the same amount again of water to each glass.

2 Trim the flower and celery stems. Stand the celery and flowers in coloured water and leave them for a few hours.

DIRTY WATER
The plants absorb the coloured water. The colouring acts like pollution. As the plants drink the water, they drink up any pollution that is in it. This happens to any person or animal that drinks polluted water.

WATER POLLUTION
Factory wastes and the run-off from chemicals cause water pollution. But a lot of pollution also starts at home.

CLEANING WATER

We expect clean water to drink whenever we turn on the tap. But because most of our drinking water comes from rivers, reservoirs and under the ground, it starts off dirty and full of germs. It has run through rocks and soil, and it contains the wastes of animals and plants and polluting chemicals. So the water that we use in our homes has to be specially cleaned at a waterworks before it reaches our taps, to make it safe to drink.
Try constructing this water filter, to find out how it is done.

A jug of water

Soil

EQUIPMENT

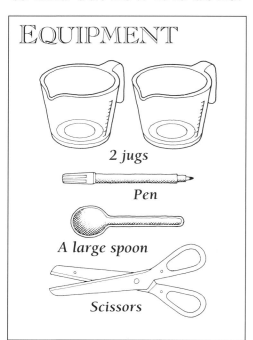

2 jugs

Pen

A large spoon

Scissors

You will need

Grass and leaves

Blotting paper

Gravel or small stones

A clean flower pot

Coarse sand

18

Making the water filter

1 Spoon some small amounts of soil, sand, gravel, grass and leaves into the jug of water. Stir everything together.

2 Stand the flower pot on the blotting paper and draw around the base of the pot. Cut the circle out of the blotting paper.

3 Put the circle of blotting paper at the bottom of the flower pot. Half fill the pot with sand, then add a layer of gravel.

Using the water filter

Stand the flower pot filter on top of an empty jug. Slowly pour the muddy water into the filter.

What happens

The water that runs out of the filter is cleaner than the water poured in because the filter traps a lot of the dirt. The filters at a waterworks are very thick and make water much cleaner. Then the water has special chemicals added to it, to kill any germs that are left.

Muddy water

Flower pot filter

The water runs out through the hole in the bottom of the flower pot filter

Cleaner, filtered water

ROTTING AWAY

Why isn't the countryside full of organic waste: dead leaves, the bodies of animals, and old trees? The test below will help you to understand how nature gets rid of and recycles its waste.

Do you ever wonder what happens to people's rubbish? Most of it is buried and cannot be recycled. Do the test at the bottom of the page to find out what happens to it.

Watch it rot!

You can do this test with a red pepper (or capsicum), or with other foods, such as a piece of bread, a small piece of cheese or an apple core.

Slice the red pepper in half (so that you can see inside it). Put half the pepper (or any other piece of food you are using) in a plastic bag and tie the top of the bag firmly. Then just leave it for a week or two.

Look at the food every day and make notes of what happens to it in your green diary (see page 44). Do not open the plastic bag and touch the food. The red pepper was photographed without its bag to make it easier to see.

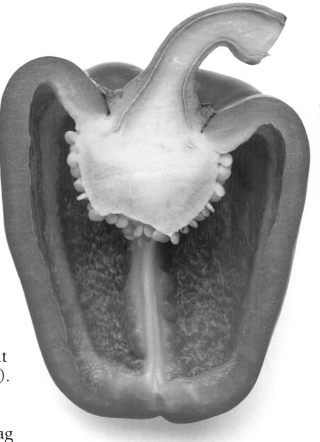

Day 1   *Day 5*

The burial test

To find out what rots down, try burying the things on the right in separate holes in the garden. Mark where the holes are, then dig the things up a month later. Which things are rotting? Turn the page to find out about recycling man-made rubbish.

A leafy twig

A polystyrene egg carton

An empty tin

NATURE'S RECYCLERS

As the days go by, the red pepper shrivels up and goes mouldy. After two weeks it has shrunk and grown lighter. What happens is that the mould actually eats the pepper. Moulds are a type of fungus. They are in the air all around you, but they are so tiny that they are invisible. Moulds land on food and eat it away. Other fungi, bacteria, and worms, mites, insects and other creatures do the same with dead plants and animals. They clear away nature's waste by breaking it down into minerals and humus in the soil, which can then be used as food by newly growing plants and animals. Things that rot down like this are said to be "biodegradable".

Day 8   Day 10   Day 15

Pieces of paper and newspaper   A piece of cotton or woollen fabric   An empty bottle   An apple core

YOUR RUBBISH

Every year the average household throws away a huge amount of rubbish - probably at least 100 dustbin-fulls. Most of it ends up on rubbish dumps or buried in pits. Either way, the enormous amount of rubbish and the nasty mixture of things that go into it are causing a huge pollution problem.

Luckily you can do a lot to help solve the problem. Most of our rubbish can be reused or *recycled*. This means that fewer new things have to be made, which saves energy and reduces pollution. Try sorting your rubbish into the groups below. At the bottom of the page you can find out what to do with them.

METALS

Magnet

Most food cans, some bottle tops and some ring pulls are made of steel. These stick to a magnet.

Aluminium does not stick to a magnet.

Steel cans can be thrown away, as they are magnetically separated from the rubbish at waste centres and sent for recycling. Sort aluminium cans out from your rubbish and take them to the nearest can bank. These are usually near big supermarkets.

GLASS

Scent bottles

Jam jar

Bottles

If bottles are returnable, return them to where you bought them so they can be reused. All other glass bottles and jars can be taken to a bottle bank for recycling. Remove all bottle tops and lids first and sort the glass into the brown, green and clear containers.

PAPER

Used envelopes and writing paper

Old magazines and papers

Cardboard

Paper is made from trees. Making new paper uses up millions of trees each year. You can help by keeping all your waste paper and taking it to the local paper skip for recycling. You can also reuse paper at home, by writing on both sides.

ORGANIC WASTE

Fruit stone

Dead leaves

Vegetable trimmings

Dead flowers

Potato peelings

Onion skins

Egg shells

Grass cuttings

Flower petals

One third of rubbish is made up of organic waste - things that are biodegradable and rot down naturally. If you have a garden, persuade your parents to keep a compost heap. All the organic waste can go on to it, and it will rot down to make fertile soil.

JUMBLE

Old clothes

Old toys in good condition

Old baby clothes

Old books

Leftover fabric and yarn

None of these things is broken or worn out, but you no longer have any use for them. Pass them on to other people who may need them, by taking them to jumble sales, charity shops, local hospitals or children's homes.

PLASTICS AND MIXED MATERIALS

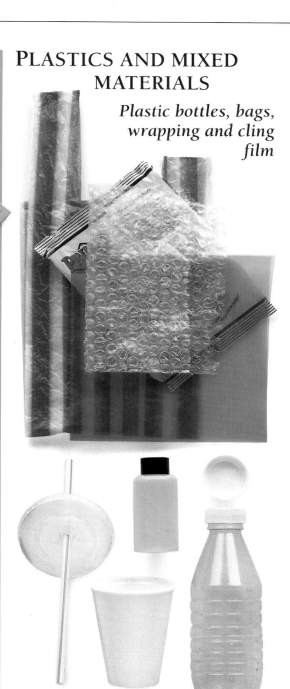

Plastic bottles, bags, wrapping and cling film

Plastic packaging

Plastics are indestructible. There is nothing much you can do to recycle them, although people are trying to find uses for them. The best way to avoid having to throw them away, is to avoid buying them in the first place.

PACKAGING

One of the main sources of everyday waste is packaging. Packaging can be useful. It protects goods and may provide useful information about them. But many things come in layers and layers of unnecessary paper, plastic and card. Usually, the more expensive a product is, the more layers of wasteful packaging it has.

The best way to reduce waste is to avoid buying anything that is overpackaged. Here you can see the amount of packaging used for a take-away meal for one child.

The packaging

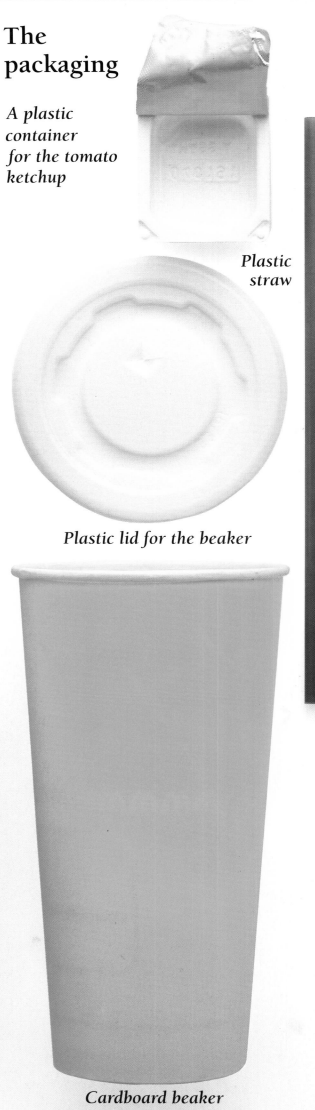

A plastic container for the tomato ketchup

Plastic straw

Plastic lid for the beaker

Cardboard beaker

The food

Tomato ketchup

A small hamburger

A small portion of chips

A cola drink

A fruit tart

Paper napkin

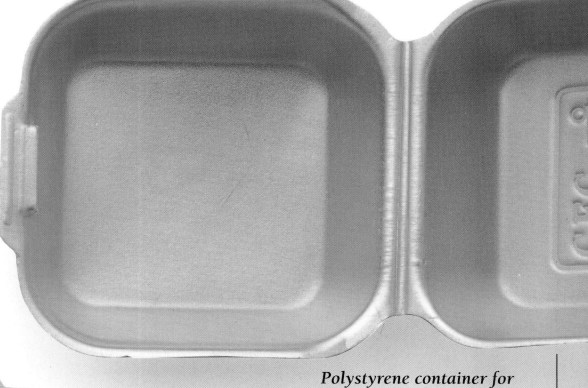

Polystyrene container for the hamburger

AVOIDING WASTE

All the packaging here will go straight into the bin. To avoid such waste, try following the points below:

- Complain about unnecessary packaging in restaurants.
- If something is overpackaged, do not buy it.
- Avoid buying small, individually wrapped items.
- Take your own bags with you when you go shopping so you do not need the endless bags that shops give out.

Cardboard container for the chips

A paper bag to put everything in

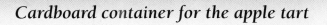

Cardboard container for the apple tart

GREEN SHOPPING

When you go shopping for food and household goods, you are faced with a huge choice of things to buy. Some of them are "greener" than others - they are better for you and less harmful to our planet. The more green products you buy, the more shops have to stock them and the cheaper they will become. Below are some guidelines on what to look for when shopping.

Wholefoods

Natural, brown rice

Refined white rice

Fresh cheese

Processed cheese

Processed food may be bleached, coloured, refined, specially packed or have had chemicals added to it. Read the labels on packages and try to avoid processed food.

Fresh is best

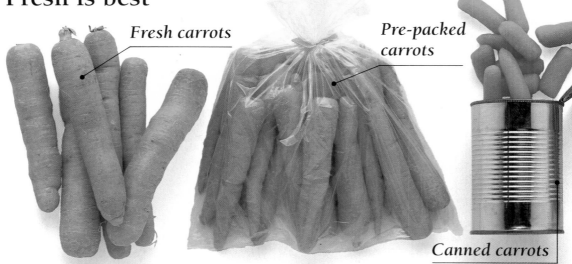

Fresh carrots

Pre-packed carrots

Canned carrots

When faced with a choice like this, go for the fresh food with the least packaging. You do not need plastic bags around everything. Tinned food, although cheap, may not be as good for you as fresh food, and its manufacture wastes both metal and fuel.

Organic produce

Organic apples

Non-organic apples, wrapped in plastic

Organic fruit and vegetables have been produced on farms that do not use chemical fertilisers or pesticides. Organic food costs more than mass-produced food, but the more of it that people buy, the cheaper and more widely available it will become.

Eggs

Free-range eggs

Battery farm eggs

Most of the hens that lay our eggs spend their entire lives in cramped wire cages. If you want to discourage this type of egg production, choose free-range eggs. These are laid by hens that are allowed space to wander. Avoid buying eggs in plastic boxes.

Recycled paper

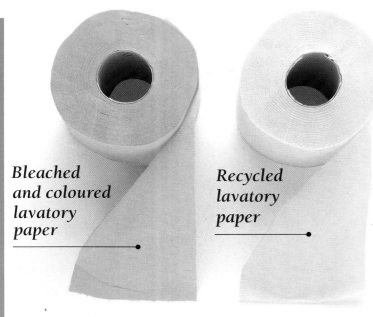

Bleached and coloured lavatory paper

Recycled lavatory paper

Bleached and coloured paper tissues

Tissues made from recycled paper

Standard pad of notepaper

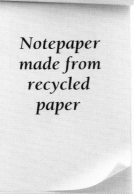

Notepaper made from recycled paper

In most supermarkets you can now buy goods made from recycled paper. They look like the things made from new paper, but no trees have been cut down to make them.

Aerosols

Aerosol spray can of deodorant

Roll-on deodorant

Most shops stock environment-friendly sprays. However, no aerosols are really green. They take a lot of energy to manufacture and have chemicals in them. Choose alternatives when you can.

Cleaning materials

Standard household cleaning liquid

Environment-friendly household cleaning liquid

You can now buy washing up liquids, washing powders and other cleaning materials that are free of harmful chemicals and strong detergents. Buying these helps to reduce water pollution.

SOIL TEST

Do you know what soil is? It is not just dirt, but a mixture of all sorts of different things. The basis of soil is finely ground up rocks and minerals from the Earth's surface. Plants, worms, insects and other creatures live on this ground up rock, then die and rot. Their remains form organic matter called *humus,* which rots down into minerals. To find out more about soil, collect as many different types as you can and do this test on them.

Different types of soil

Garden soil

You will need

A big jug of water

Farmland soil

Woodland soil

EQUIPMENT

Three jam jars

Big spoon

Pen

Labels

What to do

1 Spoon a different type of soil into each jar, until it is about a third full. Label the lid of each jar with the type of soil in it.

2 Fill the jars with water and put the lids on. Shake the jars, to mix the soil and water, then leave them to settle for a few days.

GARDEN SOIL

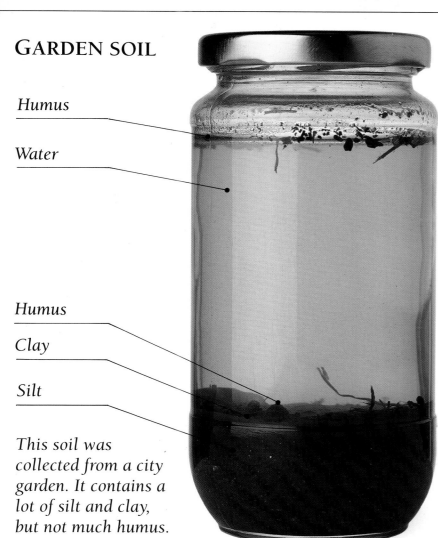

Humus

Water

Humus

Clay

Silt

This soil was collected from a city garden. It contains a lot of silt and clay, but not much humus.

FARMLAND SOIL

Humus

Water

Straw

Dead leaf

Silt

Sand

Farmland soil varies depending on the area it is in, what is being farmed and whether the farmer farms organically.

WOODLAND SOIL

Humus (leaf litter)

Water

Clay and silt

This soil was collected from an oak wood and contains a lot of leaf litter from the autumn leaves.

DIFFERENT LAYERS

After a few days, the soil in each jar settles down into different layers. The heavier parts settle first and the lightest ones - the humus - last. Look at these pictures and ask an adult to help you identify what each type of soil is made of. Then compare the soils. Which sort contains the most humus? Which sort of soil do you think plants will grow in the best? Compare soil from sand dunes or a pack of compost from a garden centre.

WHY SOIL IS IMPORTANT

Each type of soil is made up of different amounts of gravel, sand, silt, clay and humus, and different plants grow on each one. You would not expect to find the same plants growing on a sand dune and in a woodland, for example. Humus acts like a natural fertiliser and also holds soil together, so that it cannot be blown or washed away easily. Without soil, most plants could not grow. Organic gardening and farming methods take the best care of the soil, by constantly replacing its organic matter.

MAKING A WILDLIFE GARDEN

One of the best ways to help wildlife flourish close to your home is to create a special garden. You don't need much space. A window box or a large pot will do. Plant the garden with nectar-rich flowers and it will attract butterflies and bees. Here you can see how to plant a window box with late summer flowers*.

EQUIPMENT

Scissors

Watering can

Trowel

You will need

A window box or large flower pot with drainage holes in the bottom

Heather

Gravel or clay pellets

Soil-based potting compost

Marjoram (or thyme)

Sedum (Ice plant)

Chrysanthemums, asters or Michaelmas daisies

What to do

1 Fill the bottom of the window box with a layer of gravel or pellets about 3 cm deep. This lets excess water drain from the soil.

2 With the trowel, put potting compost into the window box, on top of the gravel. The window box needs to be half full.

3 Keeping the plants in their pots, decide how to arrange them. Tall plants should go at the back and trailing ones at the front.

4 Gently take the first plant out of its pot and put it in the window box. Press it slightly into the compost.

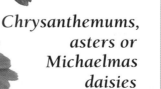

5 Do the same with the other plants. Fill potting compost in around the plants. Press it down firmly, then water it well.

For suggestions on other plants, turn to page 34.

31

WILDLIFE GARDEN

And here is the finished window box, full of flowers that will last through late summer. Put the window box on a sunny window ledge, making sure that it is stable and cannot fall. Even if you live in the heart of a city, you will be able to watch the bees and butterflies come in search of nectar. Turn the page for more ideas on plants to attract wildlife.

DAISY HEADS

Most daisy-like flowers are popular with butterflies and bees. In late summer these creatures flock to daisy-type chrysanthemums, Michaelmas daisies and sunflowers.

SWEET MARJORAM

The pink flowers of this strongly scented herb attract both bees and butterflies. Another herb that you could use is thyme, which also has small, pretty flowers.

Watering

Water the window box often enough to keep the compost moist. It will need watering every day during warm weather.

ICE PLANT (*Sedum spectabile*)

A cottage garden plant famous for attracting butterflies, the ice plant has wide heads of tightly packed tiny pink flowers in late summer. It flowers year after year.

HEATHER

This small evergreen shrub produces spikes of pink or purple bell-shaped flowers from mid-summer to late autumn. It is very popular with bees.

WINDOW BOX

This window box is made of terracotta or clay, rather than plastic. Terracotta absorbs a lot of moisture, so terracotta window boxes and flower pots need watering more often than plastic ones.

Dead heading

The plants in the window box will carry on flowering for longer if you regularly pick or snip off any dead flower heads.

PLANTS FOR THE BIRDS AND BEES

If you have a garden at home or school, there are many plants that you can grow to attract wildlife. Make sure there are plenty of spring flowers, such as aubrietia, wallflowers and honesty to provide nectar for the butterflies early in the year. A patch of stinging nettles will supply food for the caterpillars of many butterflies. Below are some good plants to grow for the birds and the bees.

HAWTHORN

Hawthorn is a wonderful hedgerow shrub for wildlife. The flowers are rich in nectar for insects, and the berries attract birds in autumn.

LAVENDER

A traditional cottage garden plant, lavender has strongly scented flowers that butterflies love.

LACECAP HYDRANGEA

Lacecap hydrangeas flower late in the summer. They have lots of tiny flowers that attract honey bees.

Buddleia

Sunflower

Sweet scabious

BLACKBERRIES

Another hedgerow plant, bramble blossom attracts bees and butterflies. Blackberries fruit in the autumn and are much loved by birds.

GIANT SEEDHEADS

Giant sunflowers are great fun to grow and in the autumn the huge, shaggy seedheads are a treasure trove for birds. They perch and sway on the dead flower heads while pecking out the oily seeds.

PYRACANTHA

Early in autumn, this striking garden shrub is laden with bright berries that birds like.

BUDDLEIA

Often called the butterfly bush, buddleia has scented flowers that attract both bees and butterflies.

SEA HOLLY (ERYNGIUM)

This is one of a family of bee plants. The thistle-like flowers appear in late summer.

Sunflower seeds

SUNFLOWER

In late summer, butterflies, bees and some small beetles are attracted to the open-faced flowers of sunflowers and other daisy-like flowers.

SWEET SCABIOUS

Attractive to bees and other insects, sweet scabious is a sweetly scented annual and flowers in summer and early autumn.

35

PLANTING A TREE

Trees are very precious. Every mature tree provides food and a home for all sorts of birds, insects and other animals. Yet every day thousands of trees are cut down for timber, to make paper*, or just to clear land for farming. We need to plant more trees - especially broad-leaved trees, which make such good homes for wildlife. Here you can learn how to plant trees of your own. On pages 38 to 41 you can find out more about why trees are vital to the health of our planet.

You will need

Different types of tree seed that you can find locally. You will need to collect these in the autumn.

Sycamore seeds

Beech nuts

Acorns from oak tree

Horse chestnuts

Seed compost

Sweet chestnuts

Gravel

On pages 38 to 41 you can find out more

EQUIPMENT

Watering can

Plant labels

Trowel

Pen

Flower pots

What to do

1 Shovel about 1 cm of gravel into the base of each flower pot. Fill the rest of each pot to just below the top with seed compost.

2 Plant a different tree seed in each flower pot. Push the seeds about 1 cm down into the seed compost. Water the compost.

3 Label each flower pot with the name of the tree. Then put the flower pots outside and wait until spring, to see which seeds grow.

Fast-growing conifers are planted specially for paper.

THE GROWING TREE

Water the flower pots regularly, to keep the compost moist. By the spring, some of the tree seeds will have started to grow. Keep a record of the trees' progress in your little green book (see page 44). Measure how fast they grow and note when they grow new leaves.

THE GROWING SEEDLING

This young sycamore tree is nearing the end of its second summer. As the tree grows, its stem becomes stronger and more woody, like a tiny trunk.

MOVING ON

Baby trees should be planted outside once they are 10 to 12 cm tall. Dig a hole in the ground a bit bigger than the pot. Take the tree and compost out of the pot and plant them in the hole.

WHERE TO PLANT?

Ask an adult where it is safe to plant your tree. It should be in a sunny but sheltered spot away from roads or buildings. Keep looking after it once it has been planted outside.

TREE TEST

Trees and other green plants play an important part in helping to keep the air around us clean and good to breathe. You have already seen how plants take in water (pages 16 and 17). Try this experiment with a tree seedling, which shows what happens to some of the water that trees drink. It also shows the fascinating effects that trees have on the climate. Then turn the page to read about the tropical rainforests and what is happening to them.

(pages 16 and 17)

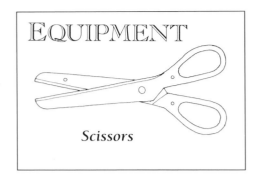

EQUIPMENT

Scissors

You will need

A large clear polythene bag

String

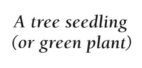

A tree seedling (or green plant)

What to do

1 Check that the tree seedling has been watered. Then carefully pull the plastic bag down over the tree, as shown.

2 Tie the plastic bag in place with a piece of string. Stand the plant on a sunny windowsill and leave for a few days.

TREE IN A WET BAG

Look at the plastic bag every day and you will soon notice drops of water collecting on the inside of it. On warm days quite a lot of water will appear. The tree has tiny holes called stomata in its leaves. Tiny droplets of water evaporate through these holes all the time, but they are so small that you cannot see them. On a hot day a big tree can lose thousands of litres of water through its leaves in this way.

BUSY LEAVES

A tree's leaves are like busy science laboratories. The tiny holes in the leaves are not just used to "sweat" out water. The tree also breathes through them.

The leaves absorb light from the sun and a gas called carbon dioxide from the air. They combine these with water to make the sugars that the tree needs in order to feed and grow.

At the same time, the leaves of the tree give off a gas called oxygen. This is very useful, as it is the gas that we and all other animals and plants need to breathe in.

SAVE TREES!

Too much carbon dioxide pollutes the air, so by absorbing carbon dioxide, trees play a vital role in keeping the air fresh. Vehicles, factories and power stations produce massive amounts of carbon dioxide by burning fuels like coal and oil. But there are no longer enough trees to absorb all the carbon dioxide. We must all try to save trees.

HOW YOU CAN HELP

- Plant and look after trees.
- Recycle all the paper you use.
- Save energy (see page 11).

TREASURES OF THE RAINFOREST

Rainforests are dense, steamy forests that grow in the tropics, where it is very hot and rains almost every day. The trees reach enormous heights and provide a home for many people and the greatest variety of plant and animal life in the world. There are so many trees that they even affect the weather. Yet people are cutting the trees down - for timber, to clear land for farming, and for roads, houses and industries. Losing the rainforests means that millions of types of plants and animals will vanish for ever. Thousands of people are losing their homes and world weather is changing. Here you can read about some of the things that come from the rainforests.

Two types of mahogany

One of the world's largest butterflies, the rare Queen Alexandra's Birdwing

PRECIOUS TREES

Many trees such as mahogany, teak and ebony, are cut down because their wood is highly valued. Help save the rainforests by persuading your family not to buy anything made of these timbers.

ENDANGERED CREATURES

The loss of animals' homes and food means that many creatures have now become extinct or, like the butterfly above, are in danger of extinction.

RARE PLANTS

Rainforest plants could be a vital source of new foods and raw materials for new medicines. As the forests are destroyed, thousands of species of plants are dying out completely.

Tropical moth orchid

MEDICINES

Thousands of rainforest plants contain things that can be used in medicines. Indeed one in four medicines available at a chemist's contains substances derived from rainforest plants.

Capsules

Cardamoms

RUBBER

Most of the world's rubber is made from white latex, which is tapped from the bark of trees that originally came from the Amazon rainforest.

Cloves

Cinnamon

Nutmegs

SPICES

Many of the main spices used in kitchens are produced from trees that come from the tropical forests. They include ginger, cloves, cinnamon, mace, nutmeg, allspice and cardamom.

Cashew nuts

NUTS

Brazil nuts come from the Amazon rainforest. The trees on which they grow have never been successfully grown in plantations, so all Brazil nuts have to be gathered from wild trees.

Brazil nuts

Pineapple

CROPS

Half of the world's main crops were originally discovered in the tropical forests. These include oranges, lemons, pineapples, coffee, rice, maize, sugar and bananas.

Vegetable oil

OILS

Many rainforest plants are rich in oils. People in the tropics use them in the same way that we use olive oil and diesel oil.

Orange

Lemon

CAMPAIGNER'S KIT

One of the best ways to help make the world a better place is to campaign to improve things. This means spreading information about what is wrong, and putting forward practical ideas on what to do about it. First, collect together some of the things shown below, to make a campaigner's kit. Over the page you can find out how to collect useful information in a special green book, and on pages 46 and 47 you can read how to set up your own campaign.

You will need

A small camera, for taking photos when conducting surveys

A notebook, for jotting down information

A pencil

Writing paper and plenty of envelopes, so that you can write letters to people who may be able to help you

An envelope file, for storing copies of your letters and useful newspaper cuttings

Coloured felt pens

Drawing pins, for pinning up campaign posters and other information (see pages 46-47)

Large pieces of coloured paper and tissue paper, to make into posters

Poster paints and a paintbrush. You need these and the felt pens for making posters for your campaigns.

Scissors

Glue stick

Card and small safety pins, to make into badges

Paper bags, for collecting samples

Sticky labels, for labelling samples that you find

Sticky tape (for badges)

43

YOUR GREEN DIARY

To become really aware of what is going on around you, keep a green diary. In your diary you can make notes of what is happening locally, keep records of your green experiments and jot down the results of any surveys you make. You can also stick in news cuttings, or seeds you find for your wildlife garden. Your green diary will be a valuable source of information if you want to set up a campaign (see over the page).

NEWS CUTTINGS

Cut out any interesting articles on green issues that you find in newspapers or magazines and stick them into your diary.

GREEN EXPERIMENTS

Make notes of exactly what happens when you do green experiments. Draw the results, or tape them into the diary, if you can.

Rain check

Made litmus paper from blotting paper. Used it to check
a) Water
b) Water and a little vinegar
c) Water and a lot of vinegar

a)

b)

Water   Acid   Strong

Tree seed

Samm 11 Whim Dm

Sycamore seeds found near Sam's house: 28:9:91

notes

Lilium tigri m spl dens. Lilium specio rubru crims

Whether you are at home, at school, out visiting or on holiday, look out for evidence of air pollution (see pages 8 to 9). Make notes of what you find and do drawings of it, if you can.

Air pollution

Have found two more samples for my pollution check: a piece of bark from Richmond park and a rock from a beach in Cornwall.

Green club

Ideas for things to make for our Green club.

membership Card

Logo for Club

CAMPAIGNING

If you are planning to start a green club or set up a campaign, you can use your green diary to make notes of your campaign points and to draw your ideas for posters, badges and cards.

Badge

Poster

45

CAMPAIGNING

The best way to improve things in the area where you live is to set up a green campaign group with friends or at school. You might want to start a litter-clearing campaign, set up a recycling scheme or create a wildlife garden. Below are some useful things for your campaign group to make.

Logo (club symbol) of row of little green people holding hands, made of folded paper.

BROCKWELL GREEN CLUB

SAVE OUR PARK

Trees made out of torn-up pieces of tissue paper glued on to the paper poster.

POSTERS

Make posters to pin up locally, so that people know what your group is campaigning for. If you are going to hold a meeting, say what the meeting is about and when and where it will be held.

Come to a meeting at Brockwell School at 5 p.m. on 26th March, 1992

46

Making badges

1 Draw a small circle for each badge you want to make on a piece of card. Use a small lid or a glass to draw around.

2 Draw a picture on each badge. Write a slogan around the picture, such as PLANT MORE TREES. Cut out the badges*.

3 Open some small safety pins. Tape the back of each safety pin to a badge, then carefully close the safety pins again.

MEMBERSHIP CARD

Make a membership card for each member of the group. Glue a passport photo of the member to the card and write on their name and the name of the group.

BADGES

Save wildlife

Stop pollution badge

Club logo badge

Save trees badge

Make a badge with the group logo on it for everyone in the group. Draw a picture on each badge and label it with the names of the group and its campaign.

WRITING LETTERS

Write letters about things that you think are wrong to the local paper, your Member of Parliament or the Prime Minister. Write your address in the top right corner of the letter, with the date beneath it. Sign and print your name at the end of the letter.

5 Rose Walk,
Brockwell
6th March 1992

Dear Sir,
I am writing to protest about the planned closure of Barnley Park. I

47

*Ask an adult to help you.

GREEN CODE

Find out as much as you can about environmental problems. Get your family and friends interested too.

Do not use the car unless you have to. Walk, cycle or use public transport.

Recycle your rubbish (see pages 22-23).

Look after your pets and plants.

Never drop litter. Pick up litter you see lying on the ground.

Do not waste electricity or water. Remember to turn off lights and taps.

Look carefully at what you buy (see pages 26-27). Avoid buying overpackaged goods, processed foods, strong chemicals or other wasteful items.

Avoid using chemical pesticides or fertilisers in your garden.

Begin a campaign to stop pollution, or save an area of wasteland for wildlife.